University of Central Florida Contemporary Poetry Series

Florida A&M University, Tallahassee
Florida Atlantic University, Boca Raton
Florida Gulf Coast University, Ft. Myers
Florida International University, Miami
Florida State University, Tallahassee
University of Central Florida, Orlando
University of Florida, Gainesville
University of North Florida, Jacksonville
University of South Florida, Tampa
University of West Florida, Pensacola

University Press of Florida
Gainesville · Tallahassee · Tampa · Boca Raton · Pensacola · Orlando · Miami · Jacksonville · Ft. Myers

Joe Survant

— **Joe Survant**

Rafting Rise

Sandy,

I hope you enjoy the "wild woman"
at the center of this book.

Joe

30 Jan. 2018

Library of Congress Cataloging-in-Publication Data
Survant, Joe, 1942–
Rafting rise / Joe Survant.
p. cm. — (University of Central Florida contemporary poetry
series)
ISBN 0-8130-2588-5 (cloth: alk. paper)
ISBN 0-8130-2589-3 (pbk.)
I. Title. II. Contemporary poetry series (Orlando, Fla.)
PS3569.U728 R34 2002
811'.54—dc21   2002027134

Frontispiece and paperback cover photo courtesy of Kentucky
Library, Western Kentucky University

The University Press of Florida is the scholarly publishing
agency for the State University System of Florida, comprising
Florida A&M University, Florida Atlantic University, Florida
Gulf Coast University, Florida International University, Florida
State University, University of Central Florida, University
of Florida, University of North Florida, University of South
Florida, and University of West Florida.

University Press of Florida
15 Northwest 15th Street
Gainesville, FL 32611–2079
http://www.upf.com

for Jeannie, once again

"They would never believe what we
could tell them. There ain't a damn
soul a-livin' around here that can back
up my tales. They's all dead now."

—L. Blackman Davison
Ohio County, Kentucky, 1978
Green River Gravel

Contents

Acknowledgments

For some of the rafting incidents and details of rafting life, I am indebted to *Green River Gravel*, a collection of historical items by Ellis and James Hartford, published by the authors in Utica, Kentucky, 1983. Certain poems originally appeared in the publications listed below.

"Rafting Rise," *The Ring of Words*, Arvon Competition anthology, United Kingdom; finalist in *The Daily Telegraph*, Arvon International Poetry Competition (1998).

"The Fiery Fox," *Kentucky Philological Review, Twenty-fifth Anniversary Chapbook* (Highland Heights, Ky.: Northern Kentucky University, 1998).

"Silver Beeches," *Kentucky Poetry Review* (Louisville: Bellarmine College, 1985), as "Arborlept."

"Bill with Horses on Jennings Creek," *Open 24 Hours* (Owensboro, Ky.: Brescia University, 1999), as "Horses on Panther Creek."

"Brother David's Warning," *Time All Over*, an anthology of the Kentucky Folk Art Center, Morehead, Kentucky (2000), as "The Prophetess of Pond River Bottoms."

"Sallie Feels Her Heaviness," *The Presence of Snow in the Tropics* (Singapore: Landmark Books, 2001), as "Maya."

Part I

1916

Brother David's Warning

She it is
comes in skunk cabbage spring
riding the spotted horse.
She it is
comes in roasting ear time
bringing whippoorwills up to the yard,
her dogs in sacks
saddlebagged behind her.

Put up your chickens,
your young pigs.
Bring the new calves
in from the fields.
She rattles
the woods on Panther Creek
and dreams the deep thickets
of Pond River bottoms.

She it is
comes in young garden time
riding the shaggy pony.
She it is
whose dogs hunt
the lower pastures
and haunt the edges
of remote farms.

Put up the fresh lambs
unsteady on their feet.
Call in your children
from the woods.
She comes riding
the blood bay mare
her hounds in bags
behind her.

Sallie Speaks of Her Calling

Words and medicine are what I bring,
loose sounds bound by rain
and dark roots dug in marshy
places when the southern wind is rising,

and lately, too, I've grown religious,
fire leaking from the body dying
since that time I lay in the woods
three days sighing with fever and chills,

the heat and cold working my body
like a rack. I would have died
if my dogs hadn't lain close around me
keeping off the chill with their warm dog-smell.

They could tell my need, and saw him too,
as he sat beside me, leaning against
an old gum that had begun to send
messages of death to the golden leaves above me.

He never spoke, but sang bits of songs
that seemed familiar, though the words were strange.
The dogs too pricked up their ears,
and Ruth whined and came and lay upon me.

He gathered twelve stones into four piles
and made a bed of saplings, then kindled
a fire from fever and motioned me to lie there,
but I was afraid, and Ruth was still upon me.

I awoke to a rising wind and Moses
coming toward me with a spring rabbit
in his jaws. The fever had passed out
of my body. Now I needed heat.

dogs named for Bible character

4 —

In my need I found a rock house and
built a fire, ripping off the rabbit's fur,
emptying guts to the dogs,
then tearing at half-cooked meat.

My stomach full, I fell into a sleep where
I stood on a hill looking over water,
watching as a cloud like a hand came
off the river and the sky blew black.

The storm woke me and I was grateful
for the deep rock ledge with its dusty
floor and scattered sandstone boulders.
The dogs came closer and lay against my back.

Since then I see what needs there are
when I come calling, men in loneliness,
women hurt with no comfort,
children worm-infested and weak.

So I bring the healing weeds and words,
fluxroot, bitterroot, archangel, feverwort,
and speak to them in tongues my
sickness taught me. I must speak

and they must listen. Sometimes, when
the second sight is on me, I say what
I'd rather not, seeing the darkness
that hangs around them.

For this they fear me, yet seek me in
the yellowing fields as I drift southward.
Drowsy in the year's last heat,
I turn away, not wanting to speak.

Sometimes, coming upon womenless shacks
in the steep and gloomy woods, I
have lain down and raised
my knees among the blueweed

and creeping jenny. For this too
I'm cursed and sought, and so,
I drift in and out of their lives
as lilies rise and fall in the ditches.

The Stranding

I. Carl Peters

Dark rain came in a blind curtain.
The river rose with a heavy breathing.
When the rain stopped, the temperature dropped
and we began freezing. Tom worked the steering
oar. The sandbar rolled its back at us,
and I shivered at the fore. Silent snags
sliced the rising river. Suddenly a tow head
reared in the dark high water. The big
raft's weight carried us way up on it
and the sudden stop threw me halfway in the water.
It was night, it was cold, and we were freezing.
We walked our raft in a figure eight
to keep from dying. Tom said if we made

a circle we'd fall down drunk
and finish freezing. So we walked all night
against the cold, but both of us were fading.
Tom stumbled and fell, I helped him up,
then I fell twice, but we went on walking.
As we walked our frozen pants
made a sound like cracking ice.
We struggled in darkness, falling,
rising, walking, until the grainy stillness
of the wood entered our feet and crept
up our legs in a dull spell.
We fell, wood on wood.
The numbness of oak was an awful blessing.

II. Bill Balcom

We came upon them
near the mouth
of South Creek,
their raft rising from
the mist, stuck tight
on a tow head.
One was dead,

the other barely breathing.
Overalls frozen
to their backs,
they lay in the track
of the figure eight
they'd worn in the bark
of the white oak and poplar

as they walked all night
to keep themselves
from freezing.
We tied our raft
to theirs and loosened
our little dinghy.
Then Robin began to row

for the wagon we saw
camped on the banks
of the Green. Carl
Peters still breathed
and I wrapped him in my coat.
Tom Simpson lay

like frozen wood
in the bottom of our boat.
We hailed the
wagon where Ben

Williams and Homer
Tracy sat by
a little fire. They
heard my call

and pulled our prow
onto the frozen
mud. We carried
them ashore and
jerked the buttons
off Carl's shirt
and Ben rubbed

him down with warm
white whiskey
while Homer built
up the fire
and the cold air
cracked and groaned
around us.

When he began
to moan, we
wrapped him up
in blankets and his blood
began to rise.
The other one lay
in a blue hard

gaze where we
had dropped him,
but the river would
not wait. We
hurried back
to our tethered raft
and went on down the river.

III. Ben Williams

Hard rain in the night and now
the spit of a little blue snow
in the breath of the freezing river.

Homer was feeding the fire
when I heard Bill cry
and saw Robin working

the oars of their dinghy.
"Ben, Homer!" Bill called.
"Build up that fire,

one's froze to his death
the other's followin' after!"
Tom Simpson was brittle and blue

but Bill held Carl
and he was breathing.
We rubbed him down

with good warm whiskey.
When he moaned and moved
we wrapped him up

and hitched the team
toward Rockport. The wagon
cracked in the cold

and the horses pulled against
each other in their traces.
The hard snow whispered as it

fell on us in the wagon
seat, and on the face
lying cold behind us.

IV. Tom Simpson

From within my wooden hull
I call to them, but the air
is freezing in my cold lungs,
thick words gum teeth and tongue.
I am learning the true nature of wood,
its dense grains, and slow time,
the way it grows around me.

They take me for a dead man.
Their words are strange now.
That life is passing, the river's quick
pulse slowing. Look for me when the
river rises in the morning sun,
but I will not be. Like a felled tree
I await the slow news of suffocation.

The Healing

I. Sallie

Homer Tracy stopped me on the road
to Sorgho, said Sam
was sick, Sarah frightened.
Would I help him if I could?

Sam was lying on a pallet
beside his mother's bed.
When I spoke he didn't
answer, or even move his head.

Sarah told me of a long
night of fever and convulsions.
Worry erased her face
and a stranger spoke to me.

I touched his head and felt the fire
rush upward through my fingers.
And I saw too a cold green
form basking in his warmth,

the weight of its dry scales pressing
on his breath and filling up his throat.
I asked for a cup of water and stirred
in snakeroot powder, then lifted

his head and made him take a drink.
All day we watched and prayed,
giving powder and prayer through the night.
At dawn his fever broke and left

him drenched in sweat. We changed
his clothes. He ate a little soup.

Outside the late January sun conjured up
the small heads of crocuses, gold, white, and purple.

II. Sarah Tracy

When Homer brought
her in, I was
too frightened
to resist him.
All night the fever
had shaken Sam
and he glowed
like a hot
coal in his bed.

"Let me see him," she said.
And I led her
to the pallet.
When Sallie spoke
Sam didn't answer.
Then she made
a little potion
from that old sack
she carries.

Sam drank.
I mopped his head,
and Sallie began
praying in a loud
voice, "Lord,
help this boy.
Drive his fever
out among the trees."
Outside her dogs were howling.

We kept it up,
a rhythm of praying,
potions, and cool bathing.
The light went.
Trees pressed in
dark and damp
around the house.
Homer built up the fire
and lit the coal oil lamp.

Near first light
I fell asleep
and dreamed that Sam
ran screaming from
the yard. "Get it off me!"
he cried. When I looked,
I saw around his neck
the body of a bright
green snake.

Then I was back
again, and looked
at Sam intently.
No snake, and his
breathing was content.
A low bright sun
drove back the trees.
Sallie turned to me,
"His fever's finally breaking."

A Visit

I asked permission to enter,
and it was given. Vida Couch gave me
a seat before the fire to drive
away the damp. I gave her sassafras

and she turned up the lamp, but she was ill
and soon went up to bed. I sat apart
from John and the children, looking
into the fire until the room fled

and the voices of the children
blended with the fire's noise
in stops and starts and popping.
All the while its insistent sigh

ran on beneath the flames and
entered my head and coiled itself
within me. Then noise stopped
altogether and I saw the signing

of the fire, the V it made, blue
rising into orange and yellow.
Then I knew she'd die and
turned myself out into the cold

morning and walked through the muddy
field where young corn had not yet
grown and the gray wet clay
clung to my boots like stone.

At the Camp Meeting

I. Susan Rose

I knew he'd come
so I put on my yellow
dress and combed
rosewater through my hair.
I studied him secretly,
learning his lean strong limbs
as he moved among the crowd.
When I saw him take
a piece of the buttermilk
pie I'd baked,
I looked straight at him
and he at me. My
face felt warm, but

I didn't look away.
Brother David began
to speak and everyone
moved up around him,
but I hung back and
stepped into the woods
and followed a little trail
hardly worn at all
until I came to an
open place where the tall
trees held off the brush
and made a little cove.
Bill entered through
the trees and all
the birds were hushed.

He just came up
and kissed me
where I stood.

Little cared I for
camp meetings then,
and I raised my arms
to hold him
and kissed him back.
Behind us the singing
had begun, sending
out the old question
among the oak and swaying gum,
"Shall we gather at the river?"
And we did.

II. Bill Balcom

When I took
a piece of Susie's
buttermilk pie,
I saw her looking,
and when I ate
I imagined
her taste.

I looked and ate,
humming with hunger.
The meeting flowed
around us, but
she didn't look away,
then drifted out
on the crowd's edge.

I watched her
yellow dress
disappear in the woods
like the raised flag
of a fleeing deer,
then circled around
before her.

We met
in a little clearing.
Neither of us spoke,
just came together.
I kissed her there and
she kissed me, then
undid her long black hair.

Among the Weeds

Weeds with their green strangled hunger
have their own schemes plotted in tight
lean rooms whose secrets I can
never learn. In their prickly clothes

they come into our gardens and pastures.
Horseweed ten feet tall in the meadow
still thrives and redoes itself
at four inches in the hard horse lot,

while fleabane flourishes in the
crevices of boulders, and chicory raises
its blue sails on the gravelly
shoulders of roads. The slightest

breeze sets off their seeds,
clouds of yellow dust
drifting in the air. Sticktights with
their devilish faces prong my clothes

and cockleburs wind themselves
relentlessly in the feathering of Ruth's
four legs. At night I hear
their thin cries as they struggle

for their places in the ground. We pull
and chop at them, but each piece
survives and multiplies, or lies asleep
waiting its turn to come round.

Bill and Robin at the Dance

It was a late spring
night. The banks
drooped with light
green leaves, a full
moon rising, so I
agreed when Robin said
to keep on running.

We entered the
Green that morning
and passed through
Rumsey Dam.
Now we rode
on the river's back
down to the big Ohio.

I took the oar
while Robin slept,
and lit my pipe
and watched the
shore go by
with Susie Rose
on my mind.

Around ten, at
the big bend
near Birk City
a whirlpool
caught us
and turned us
in lazy circles.

Round and round
we went for hours,
while high on the bank

above us was
a big house
with a square
dance progressing.

Robin slept,
the raft turned.
I listened to
the music and
heard the calls
and thought some
more of Susie.

When we broke
free I took
the oar to keep
us off the bank.
I let Robin sleep
and went on
with my musing.

After light I
woke Robin and
hoped to sleep awhile.
He raised up and said,
"Bill, you know, at every house
we passed last night,
they was dancing."

Bill with Horses on Jennings Creek

They stand
at the far end
of the field, just
up from the creek
where Johnson grass
grows shoulder high
and cool air

flows up
from the water.
The black sees me
first. He shakes
his head. The mares
neigh welcomes.
They trot, then

gallop, now run
toward me. I want
to speak. They
clench and unclench
like great fists.
They ripple with light
as they come from the shade.

I envy their strong
impossible bodies.
The air is filled
with their greetings.
I want to answer,
but how to speak
and what to say?

Sallie Feels Her Heaviness

The cattle stand facing east.
They shine like lumps
of coal in the rising sun.
I stand in the center of the worn

geometry of their paths. Sun
warms their black hides, making
light upon them tremble.
Hard hooves have vanished.

Around me the yellow heads
of dandelions collapse and rid
themselves of ragged bodies
rising from milky roots.

Nearby the tight brown coats of
cattails emphatic on the margins
of the pond have begun to dissolve
into flakes of airborne down.

Here in Ben Williams' low pasture I watch,
wearing my heaviness like a coat.
Hard matter in its home around
me seems poised to disappear.

Wild Grapes

We followed him
through woods of winding,
gloomy ways
with no relief from green,
and the deep trees made
a permanent screen
above us, silence
broken only by
our breathing. Now and
then a fox squirrel
twitched his bright
bush and fussed at us,
or a redheaded woodpecker
swooped off screaming at our

intrusion. We were
hunting sweet wild
grapes in Rough
River bottoms.
The way was twisting,
but Bill knew where to find them.
He led the way with
Jenny and me behind him.
We had gone beyond
the woods I knew to find
the sweetest grapes
and eat them. As we
walked, Jenny and I talked
and ate of those we'd gathered.

We'd fallen behind
laughing at the stains
upon our lips when

we heard someone calling
from the rising just behind us.
The voice was muffled
by all the leaves, so we
stopped and looked around us.
It came again and I
knew that it was
Carl Peters. Jenny
frowned and said,
"Do you hear that, Susie?
I broke off with him."

Then she turned and ran
where he was calling
from a stand of oak and
walnut. I caught up
with Bill and took
his hand. We heard
Carl yell and
Jenny scream,
and a pistol's noise
broke up the bottom's
muggy silence.
I called to Jenny and
we ran toward the shot.
Then we heard another.

We found them lying
in a little pool of light
where the forest's roof had
opened up a place to let
in the tangled undergrowth.
Carl was propped against
an oak, the revolver lay
beside him. I went to
Jenny and raised her up.

She was limp against me.
The apron she wore was soaked
in blood, but all I could see
were her cooling lips still stained
with the grapes' wild juices.

Haying

I came upon them in hard September
haying in a field beside the road,
John Couch, Lou Verst, and Homer Tracy.
Around us summer in her last days

let go her heat and the locusts
raised their old complaint about
the coming cold. Steadily they sawed
in the trees and the air was still.

I did not speak but watched them work
from under the big white oak
that put its shade like a hand
against the hard dry heat.

No sound but the insects and Homer
calling to the horses as they drew
the mower through the grass,
the sweet smell of its death sent

out by the softly whirling blades.
Then a cloud passed over us
rising suddenly out of the empty sky,
and I saw it had the shape of a man.

Despite the fine blue day
I could not help myself
and cried out, "This afternoon
one of you will die!"

They looked at me uneasily
but did not speak. I rose and
went away but heard the news
next day, how Homer riding the high

load to the barn was tricked
by the wagon's sway, falling headfirst
to the hard ground. My words rose up
in my throat like hot gorge and I

could not speak, while all around
me the unmoved cicadas cast off
the brittle shell of their old selves
and sounded their shrill, unbroken warning.

The Warning

Loosestrife has escaped its limestone
wall and come into the yard
raising its purple spikes, signaling
in the fescue. Wild grapevines roam

the woods making their final choices.
The thicket is lit by blazing star
and trumpetweed's dull glow
flickers in the fallen leaves.

Their stubborn lives have occupied
the marshy floor. More and more
I see their insistent purple
flowers, feel their quick fire

burning like memory underground.
Loosestrife is in our yards
and at our doors. "Live," it whispers
in our sleep, "I'm coming."

Bindweed

I was in the Balcoms' garden
picking through late fall's leavings.
The cool smooth hulls of watermelons
rose out of the dying weeds like slow

green turtles surfacing all around me,
and the red cheeks of tomatoes grinned
cheerfully at my labor. A few pumpkin
squash, an ear or two of small late

corn, the untroubled geese calling
above me, when all at once
I heard a soft buzzing noise
like the stumbling of a dying horse.

The sound entered my head
and stopped me. I fell down
among the hills of exhausted squash
in the little valleys invaded

by bindweed that hugged the ground
and pulled the pole beans down,
then turned upon me its blank white
faces and empty purple eyes.

Charity

I. Tilda Verst

"I swear I saw her sacrificing a chicken this
morning! It was by that crop of big boulders
down where Jennings Creek bends back and
almost touches itself. There she was, blood on
her face, the bird flopping and spraying all over
her arm and dress. Her dogs just sat there
watching, and while she held it, she muttered
a terrible curse. I half thought to see Satan him-
self rise up out of the water, or one of those
dogs change its shape and drag her down. I tell
you, Lou Verst, I can't believe we've let her
sleep on our kitchen floor, not ten feet from our
bed. And when I think of the children . . . well,
I can't! Don't let that softness in you take pity
next time she asks to come inside. We'll give
her and those mangy dogs some food and send
her on her way. Someone else can take her in."

II. Lou Verst

I saw her coming through the cut
and knew Tilda would be
looking for some excuse when
she heard Sallie had taken up
with Ben Williams again, maybe
even making it up as she went.
No doubt she did see Sallie
cleaning a chicken down
by that rockhouse where
she sometimes sleeps when
no one will take her in.
I don't know how she
lives when the fits are

on her, driving her out of charity
in all kinds of weather. If it
weren't for those dogs of hers . . .
It's the damnedest thing
I've ever seen, the way they share
their hunt with her, spooky
to those like Tilda that have never
gotten close to dogs. I expect
old Queenie would share with me
the way she puts a quail in my
hand despite her hunger in a
long day's hunt.

I walk out to meet her
away from the house,
her dogs stiffen at me,
then relent when they smell
the ham, and the pan bread
still is warm. I start
to warn her away
but she isn't listening,
mumbling something about
the sound of wings. She
looks past me at the air. I turn,
but do not see or hear a thing.
The night chill settles on our
shoulders. I see her tired clothes
and her eyes full of madness,
but who am I to say she
does not speak with God?
So I turn her away from the road
and lead her to the barn and give
her a horse blanket and a bed
of straw. Above us the roosting
pigeons jostle for their places,
their burbling makes the sound
of water over rocks as night
rises up around us.

Tongues of Light

This morning the voices were clanging
bells within me, and each one
brought a face, some frowning, some grinning,
until I could neither hear nor see

what was around me, the soughing wind
in the trees, the graceful turn of the leaves.
I was sucked into myself. The world
and all its pieces disappeared.

The voices all spoke at once
and the faces crowded inside me.
They called in the names of confusion,
in words like swarming bees

until one said softer than the rest,
"Open your ears to hear, your eyes to see."
Then I heard the forest burning with
its million leaves turning like the pages

of a book. And as I looked
I heard the subtle tongues of light,
the meanings of the leaves as they said,
"Yellow, orange, red."

The Golden Circumstance

I saw Autumn coming toward me
in a golden dress green hemmed,
with scarlet petticoat. I looked
right through her and saw the old forest

inside her trees. I looked and
I was she. I heard then the
ancient languages of elms about
to be forgotten and the words of men

already fallen from memory.
Around me the urgent voices
of sapling redbuds and sassafras
were like a choir of locusts. I felt

the dying maple blaze in the distance
and smelled the dark wet ashes
of the earth. I tasted winter in
my mouth like a strong lover.

Then I began to turn and dance
within my golden circumstance.

The Iron Castle

I had hoped to shelter tonight
with Sarah. The warm days are
dying and their heat has begun
to rise up from the earth

drawn into the empty bellies
of deep cold stars. But she
lied uneasily about having no room,
a visiting cousin she said,

though I know it's me she fears.
My head is filled more and more
with a swarm of voices that distracts me,
cutting off those I wander among.

Often when the clatter ceases
I find myself in someone's home,
the family watching, quiet and uneasy
and I wonder how long I've been gone.

Tonight I burrow deep within
her haystack and bring my dogs
in behind me, a warm enough
bed for almost any night.

The decaying hay and warm dog
bodies make a strong incense that
settles inside my head, setting
off whispering and lighting up my

dark tunnel with a fitful flare.
I see myself locked naked in a stone
house under a glaring heatless light.
Distant human voices blow

across my body like a north wind.
I reach out to myself through
the tunnel but my bodies
shrink away and cannot touch.

With sunrise my dogs and I
crawl into the weak young day,
the dogs to hunt the fields
for food, though I'll go

on down to Ben's to ask
for some milk and biscuits.
But the night still lies heavy
on my sight and I can hear

the soft gurgling sounds of those
cold voices and smell the
cold wires and see my jewel
burning inside an iron castle.

Ben Williams

After Ben took me in and fed me,
after the food had done its work,
after the November chill had fallen
from me like a cloak, I saw

him looking from his loneliness
in the dreary cabin filled with
the careless male clutter of old pans,
newspapers, and sad steel traps.

We came together hard, as though
we meant to fight, and I stepped
away from myself and watched us
rooting and rolling on his dirty pallet,

him smelling like the skins of animals,
me of dogs. But the friction of our struggle
warmed us and flared up for a minute
in the cold room, sending out a brief

sulphurous light. Later we dressed
with no shame. Ben talked a little
of the coming winter, the trapping season,
my need for shelter, the scarcity of mink.

He asked me to stay, and I did,
for a few weeks, then the voices
within me began a roaring sound
and I could not hear him speak.

The clattering tongues rang
without mercy and threw off visions
quicker than shadows rising
from a fire on long winter nights.

One grew louder than the rest,
neither man's nor woman's voice
it had a sexless trill, like some
large, strong bird mouthing

almost human words with its hard
stiff tongue. And I saw a great
flock of crows rising from the broken
corn in a whirlwind, their voices

hoarse with urgency swirling through
the brittle limbs of leafless trees.
I broke from the cabin then and ran
with Babel buzzing within me.

Timbering

I. Bill Balcom

When I looked
she was there
so sudden I
dropped my end
of the big saw
as we lifted it
against the oak.

Robin turned as Sallie
spoke, asking us
not to cut the tree.
We laughed uneasily,
something about her
sudden dark clothes
beside the silver beech.

The sycamores lifted
their white arms above us
and we saw the thickness
of the oak. We didn't
answer but together
moved over to a
shag bark hickory.

She watched for
a while as we worked.
When I looked again
she was gone. We
filled the empty afternoon
with the saw's wheeze
and the sudden deaths of trees.

II. Sallie

I asked them not to cut the big oak
but did not say it spoke to me.
They were just boys, their
minds filled with thrills on the

high water to come, and the pleasures
of Evansville. Out logging in November
Robin and Bill, full of their young
lives, had no time for me

and my nonsense about a tree.
Yet something held their hands
and they passed on by the oak
and went to work on a shaggy

hickory. I sat down to watch,
this had been my woods, a patch
of virgin trees along Rough River
in Eb Balcom's good bottom land.

The white oak, largest of them all,
stood like a bull among the long
graceful necks of water-loving
sycamores grazing by the creek,

while all around us thick, pale
beeches murmured in their slow
tongue of what was happening,
and what was yet to come.

Silver Beeches

I dream of silver-bodied
beeches. One reaches out
for me, takes me into its bole.
The dense wet grain's as sweet

as honey, and slower. The bark seals
the wound, covers the knot of hair
and bone. Years later squirrel hunters
will notice the blister on the tree's body,

remark its strange shape. And I,
like a wen in the tree's side,
will forget more and more the earth's
floor, wait to be born in blossom

and bole, yearn for the slow
secret life to come.

A Brother's Dying

A few of this year's
tough oak leaves still
rattled in the branches.
Mama and I were washing
clothes in a tub when Bob
came in from Owensboro
smelling of sour mash
from his job at Medley Distillery.
We hadn't expected him
at all, and his face
was white. Mama said,
"Susie Rose, warm your
brother some soup."
And I hurried.

He wasn't feeling well
but tried to eat and couldn't.
Suddenly he stood up
holding his stomach and
vomited blood into our
washing tub, then knelt
on the poplar floor.
Mama put a wet cloth to his
head as he heaved
more blood. The water
in the tub turned red.
"Susie Rose, go quick
for the doctor," she said.
I grabbed my shawl and ran.

When we got back
the vomiting had stopped,
so we put him in Mama's bed.
I took off his boots
while Mama wiped his head.

"He's bleeding inside," Dr. Rayburn said,
"but now it seems to have stopped.
Keep ice on his stomach.
Nothing to eat or drink.
I'll be back tomorrow."
Mama sat with him
through the night then wakened
me to sit by him
in the cold morning light.

"Sis," he said, "I'm awful thirsty,
bring me a drink of water."
His pleas grew stronger until
I couldn't stand it and
went to get our mother.
When we came back he was
eating ice from the bag
we'd laid across his stomach.
"A little ice won't hurt," said Mama.
As the day grew brighter, he looked at us,
"Is it getting night already?"
"No," Mama said, and opened up the curtain.
Bob closed his eyes and breathed once deeply,
then looked like he was only sleeping.

The Trotline

Driven by a chorus of voices,
I wandered away from familiar trees
and fields, deep into fall,
up the river in its sullen winding.

Up the Green in its autumn dropping,
its blank surface cluttered with the trees'
debris as they shake off summer
before the late rains come

to bring the rising current that licks
the channel clean and slicks down
the banks with sleek gray mud,
and leaves surprises of driftwood

clustered like dusty fruit forty
feet up the pale trunks of sycamores
clutching at undercutting banks
the river devours in long, slow meals.

For seven days I wandered, now
and then entering invisible cold rooms
made strange by the muggy air around
them. Moses and Ruth ranged the bottoms

before me. The land on the opposite side
rose high in sandstone cliffs, game
grew scarce. Streams often
disappeared into holes. The land was hollow

below me. The river deepened,
falling into a dark green gloom.
Hunger led us to the river, despite
my dread of bottomless water.

I found a little skiff hidden
near a maple where a trotline stretched
out into the river. My dogs whined and
paced about, but didn't try to follow

as I stepped into the boat and picked
up the mossy cord where it met
the water and slanted down beyond my sight.
Slowly I pulled myself along the line.

The boat moved easily. There was hardly
any current. The river put all its effort
into going down, and the trotline followed.
As I pulled, the line rose and smaller

twine with baited hooks hung down
every foot or so. Carefully I raised it up
avoiding the barbs and the chicken guts
they carried. Something tugged on

the line, then a catfish rose
struggling toward me. It turned
and twisted in the green water and, ugh,
for a second it looked like a baby!

I lifted it into the boat and cut
the twine free of the line. It fell
flopping and gasping at my feet.
One more like this I thought

and we'll have our first true meal
in a week. Now the line seemed hung.
I tugged but the snag held
and the boat's bow dipped down.

In dread of the cold deep water
I let go, but the line caught
on an oarlock, and then began to move.
I pulled on the line to lift it

and felt a slow heavy life
below me. Something powerful swam
away from the boat, and it tipped even more
with the strain. I reached with my knife

to free me, but fumbled it into the stream.
In my panic I grabbed the line
and leaned against the tilt and
pulled as hard as I could.

The line gave and something rose
toward me in the deep water.
Again I pulled the boat along
avoiding the swinging hooks.

Then the line moved against
me, burning out of my hands.
Twice it turned, but the third time
I pulled it gave again

and a great yellow catfish came
toward me, swimming in a greenish light.
It was half as big as the boat.
I stopped, and it hung in the water.

Its blank muddy eyes had nothing
to do with me or my world.
It floated calmly and looked at me.
Its spines stuck out like horns.

The small twine snapped. The fish
lay still for a moment, then was gone.
I dropped the line and fell down,
blind in the bottom of the boat.

I felt this slow world speed
up. The shadows of trees flashed
like sudden lightning strokes across
the boat. The river ate away its banks

in a quick fit of gluttony. Maples and sycamores
fell into the water, were carried away,
then reborn in green saplings that
rose and fell in their turns.

The river deepened, the cliffs rose
then crumbled, refilling the river's bed.
I felt the boat drawn down
as the river dropped into the ground.

The air grew cold, there was a roaring sound.
I awoke screaming with Moses and
Ruth licking me and whining.
I was myself again. The skiff

had drifted back to shore. The catfish
had stopped its flopping and lay still
beside me in the boat. I got up then
and ran, far away from the river.

Robin Floyd Remembers His First Trip

I was pulling the stern oar.
Dad was piloting. We'd been out a while
when we struck a hidden rock.
My oar swung round
and threw me in the river. I
struggled to rise, but the raft was running
above me. When I popped up
behind the logs, Dad threw me
a rope and we kept on running. But I
wasn't strong enough to handle an oar,
and we took a terrible pounding
at Drum's Back Rock, then
the current swept us against Blue
Bluff. Daddy said, "Pull
the oar, boy!" and I tried
but couldn't. The raft hit the bluff
and the current held us and beat us
against it. The raft was coming apart
so I jumped and swam hard
to the roots of a big sycamore
standing on the other side. I
climbed out in the cold and saw
Daddy still on the heaving raft.
I yelled, "Get off there,
Dad, it's breaking!"
But the logs he stood on parted
and he went down between them.
I yelled again and he
came up swimming. The river
swept him along and I followed
running. I met him at the bank
and the raft went on down
the river. We watched it go

then hurried to warm ourselves
in my uncle's house a mile
up Wolf Pen Creek.
It was my first trip.
Already I was in love with the river.

— Part II

1917

The Fiery Fox

I found a fiery fox bleeding
in a stump and took him home
and rubbed his damp fur until
he began to glow and burn.

Steam rose from him in a cloud.
His bloody coat smelled of pine.
No, it was not a fox fiercer
than the fire burning in my room.

An owl with a broken wing
hopped across my sandy floor
with clouds of blood and rain,
filling the rocky room with the deaths

of tender rabbits and softly fluttering
birds and nights of silent wings.
No, it was not a fox or owl
I heard thumping in the dark.

The wind came up and rattled
the empty trees. I looked and looked
but could not see a face
or even say a name.

The Soggy Woods Release Their Sorrow

The dull winter drizzle stirs
the fever in my bones and drives
me out of my stony home in the deep
and lonely woods. I slink wet

with my hounds to Ben's front door.
"Come on in, Sal," he says,
"it's a mite damp out there."
Soon the musty perfume of wet dog

hair heating before the fire
fills the room. I ask for water
and a cloth, then push the dogs
aside, undo the buttons of my shirt.

The fire hums its warming song.
Ben is all attention.
He touches my bare shoulders
and I slowly turn around.

The voices are silent now.
The soggy woods release their sorrow
in a mist that fills the air. We come
together. Outside the trees are bare.

The Plumb Line

I. Sallie

When the wind dropped and the sky
cleared, the little heat of the earth
began to drift into the spaces high
above me. The cold settled down

like perfectly fitted clothes, and I knew
I had to find shelter. Even Moses
and Ruth shivered and pressed against me.
I came to the Balcoms' place just as

the winter sun rolled on its side
and sank beneath the hills.
They with their good hearts, I knew
they'd take me in. I hadn't seen

Bill for about a month or so
since I came upon him and Robin
cutting timber in my grove.
Now he hardly spoke to me,

smarting from male pride at my
staying of his hand, though it was
not me, I did but ask,
he and Robin did but agree.

Laura and I talked by the fire.
I told her of Edna's illness
and Opal's quick delivery of her
second child, but while we talked

my voices also began to speak,
murmuring like coming rain
breaking around my voice and hers
until I must strain to hear

what they would say. In silence I
prayed but they overwhelmed
my prayer and spoke clearly
without words, pictures swarming around

my brain making a weeping sound.
As I sat before the fire, I was
afraid and resolved not to speak,
but Laura saw the fear in my silence.

I watched it flow across the floor
and lie like a heavy fog between us.
It entered her body like poisoned
air, she sagged and her eyes

were brittle glass. I left
before dawn, slipping down
to the barn to whistle up my dogs,
my pockets full of last night's biscuits.

The low winter sun did its best
to burn away the frost.
I could feel it on my face,
but was lost inside myself

and would have no part of sun,
but kept counsel with the frozen
weeds giving up their ruptured
hearts beside the frozen road.

II. Laura Balcom

Though I felt sorry
for the poor old thing
I didn't like the way
she looked around so blankly,
and remembered, too,
about Homer Tracy

last fall. John and Lou
swore that she had
cursed him. I doubt it.
Still and all, the way she looks

when I catch her eyes,
as if she wants to speak
but can't. If only Robin had not
come by for Bill that November
day with his stories of adventure
on the flooded river and money
from the timber, and high times
in Evansville. They
cut and hauled logs all
December, then cobbled

together a raft, now
await the rafting rise
when the first rains of February
gather in Rough River
to push the banks aside
and float the channel free.
I know he's almost
grown and Eb says
to cut him loose
and let him be a man,

but he worries too.
Sallie came to the house
at supper time. It was
so cold even her dogs
looked stiff. We took her
in and I was glad for
a woman's company,
news of my neighbors,
who was sick
and who in labor.

Later I noticed
a change, her brooding,
and her quiet. How she
seemed to listen
not to us, for she hardly
spoke and would not
answer or look at me.
That night she sat in a
vacant mood looking in
the fire, listening to

something in her head.
Next day she slipped
away before I rose
in the dead gray light.
I was relieved but
could not shake the
fear that hung like
hoarfrost in my
kitchen and put a
friction in my chores.

III. Sallie

I walked alone in Laura's garden
on paths worn through dead Johnson
grass and frozen stalks of corn
whose brittle arms rattled as I passed.

The dread that came over me in Laura's
house still clung like lichen
and the stink of woodsmoke rising
from the fire in my stony kitchen.

The voices died down but a man
followed after, a stranger though
I could not see his face or hands.
Suddenly he was before me.

In a long coat beside the stacked
stone wall he held a plumb
line out and looked at me.
I felt the strict measure

of the string go taut in my breast,
deeper than bone, and the garden
and the wall shifted westward.
The river turned in its hard bed
and the garden lost all of its focus.

Susan Rose's Plea

I asked him not to go.
I couldn't take
another death, first
Bob, then Jenny, but
there's a wildness in him
and Mama said I'd best
let him break it.
I had seen the swift
water rising up the banks
like cold breath, and I'd heard
the tales when the men
were talking, of rafts
come apart on Drum's Back Rock
high in the freezing water.

Oh, he listened as
I spoke, and wanted
to please me, but Robin
and the river were waiting,
and I knew I couldn't
talk him out of his pride
and hunger for high adventure.
Maybe I wouldn't want him
if I could. He's like the hidden
wire in me, coiled
tight with desire for living.
I just wish he'd wait for late spring
when the water is just as high,
but far more forgiving.

The Feast

It was a feasting table and many
sat around it. Some faces seemed familiar,
yet changed to the faces of strangers
when I looked more clearly.

My mother gone thirty-five
years sat beside me and wept
when I looked at her, and the ten
year old I was when she died

sat on her other side, unaware
and smiling. Across from me
the father I never knew
took up his fork and began signing.

I tried to speak to them
but couldn't. Their lost voices
were muted and wooden. The smell
of damp bark lay about them.

A man who looked like Homer Tracy
stood up and said, "Eat of this meat
those of you who still remember
your bodies, what your lives

once were, and their passing."
We began to eat, but the taste
was bitter and the bite I'd taken
came up with bile from my stomach.

I saw the roasted venison
on its platter and my hands began shaking.
Someone passed around the head
in a covered dish. When I lifted

the lid, it was Ruth's. I stood
up from the table screaming
while the others lifted glasses of
ruby wine, and went on eating.

Bill Waiting

It has rained
for three days,
first in blind
curtains, now
in a slow drizzle.
Bear Run and
Grassy Creek

feed into the Rough
and push it up
uncertain banks.
Tomorrow will bring
the rise when
the raft will lift
up on the tide

and we will
ride it down
to Evansville.
I promised
Susie I'd take
the money I make
and put it back

for our future.
Now I lie
in my bed without
sleeping, hearing
the rain in its
ceasing, feeling the
cold behind it.

I dream
I'm already
on the river,

the raft lifted up
in a great hand,
Robin and I
struggling to steer it.

The water drops
away and I am
alone in a frozen
woods, stalked
by an unseen animal.
I run, it
follows. I hear

the clicking sound
of claws
on frozen ground.
I awake in the hesitant
light, sleet rattling
against my window.
There's Robin's whistle!

Second Sight

I felt the hand of God
in my head, His voice driving
out the others, then the sudden fit
was on me. I fell down

in Lou Verst's dark woods
and rolled about the ground.
Then all was quiet. I lay
like death, and my dogs were still.

I saw a great black wagon
filled with the bodies of men I knew
rolling through a strange pasture,
their faces like frozen ruptured weeds,

their hard lips blue with terrible
kisses. With every turn of the wagon's
wheels a blood broth surged and
stained their chins like old men's

drivel. The sound of the wheels was
continuous thunder. The light around
them was green as spring, but
the air flowed by like angry hornets.

Then I was lifted up and saw
a whole army of wagons full
of their terrible cargo stacked up
like cordwood or the carcasses of animals.

I awoke to Ruth licking my face
and whining. Above me a maple
lifted empty arms to a sky
as gray as the mud beneath me.

Rafting Rise

We came to the end
of cutting and hauling
having had enough
of wet bottoms
and yokes of oxen
up to their knees in mud,
pulling at the logs.

We came to the end
of cutting and hauling
when we saw the
great white oak
standing before us
thicker than four
could reach around.

We waited
for the rise,
when Rough River
would swell up
and fill itself,
two-thirds bank,
not too high.

We waited
beside the cold
muddy water
while the creeks
cried out,
emptying themselves
in the swelling river.

We measured time
by the river's rise

and by the sledge's
swing as we beat
together our raft
with green hickory
pins and poles.

When we first
felt the water and
the current took us,
the logs moaned,
my stomach cut loose
from my body and
floated free with the raft.

Holding the steering oar
was like fighting a great
fish when you
give it line
lest it break away,
yet try to keep it
free from stumps and snags.

The raft pulled and yawed
like it was alive,
but it was the river
that lived. We rode
on its back at the mercy
of cold water
and colder wind.

It was then I cursed
Robin who'd come
by that November day
when my father and I
were firing tobacco
in the barn.
"Hey, Bill, let's go

for the rafting rise.
We'll cut our trees
and ride them all the
way to Evansville
and sell them,
then lie up in the
Acme Hotel and Oyster Bar,

with its fifty-cent rooms
and two-dollar whores."
So I left my father
and the curing weed
and went across the
river and engaged in
cutting and hauling logs.

Now on the rising
stream, my hands
frozen to the oar,
my ears drummed
as I heard the river
roar at Falls-of-Rough
hiding around a bend.

The first logs rode over
then dipped down
into the white water
rushing below the dam.
Robin was up to his
knees while I was
lifted high. The raft

groaned like our barn
in a wind, but the
pins held and
we floated free.
Robin's pants froze and

the wind passed through
my clothes like a knife.

At Livermore we
reached the Green
and stopped awhile
to join our raft
to others—
Lou's, John's,
and Ben's.

The marshal came down
to our camp and
warned us off from town,
but Robin gave him
a bottle and we all
got drunk, forgetting
about the Green

rising up beside us
and the cold
entering our bodies
through our sodden clothes.
That night I dreamed
a late dream
of the warm barn

and the sweet smell
of smoke rising up
around the dry
bodies of curing
leaves, but awoke
cold and sick, here
on the frozen bank.

Five of us
now cut loose our

raft of a thousand logs
and headed down the Green.
If I had thought that once
we navigated the Rough
and jumped its dams

and missed the rocks
at Fishtrap and the Narrows
and joined with other rafts
then entered the broader Green,
if I had thought that
we had passed the worst,
I had not felt the

power of the Green
in full flood.
Chafing in my mother's kitchen
I could not have believed
how the wind could strike you
fair at ten above
out on the open water.

In the first night's tie-up
we took true
measure of the raft's
weight and the current's power.
In the late winter light
Ben took the skiff
and rowed off

to get a line on
a maple up ahead.
The tree gave way
and almost swamped
his little boat.
Three times he tried,
the third tree held.

Lou wrapped
our end around
the checking port when,
slowed by the cold,
his hand
fed itself
to the hungry rope

just as the raft
swung against
the current. The frozen
rope snapped taut,
hard as iron,
and Lou's hand
dropped to the deck

cleanly cut as
by an axe.
He dropped too,
his face white
as the sycamore
that held and drew us
back against the bank.

We bound his wrist
to stop the blood and
put him in our little hut.
But we could not stop
and cut the rope for
the river was on the rise
and Rumsey Dam roared up ahead.

The river ran high,
but the big dam held
its place and made
a falls that turned
the river white.

Our bow dropped down
and disappeared.

Robin and John scrambled
toward me,
up the sloping deck.
Ben and I
held on
to the oar
while the stern

reared up in the
frozen air. Again
our good hickory
poles and pins
held tight, though
the raft made
an awful sound.

We ran that day and
night while Lou
moaned in the shed.
The river ate
its muddy banks and
slowly crept
through the drowning fields.

I took my meal
of cold hard meat
at the struggling oar
wrapped in a frozen
quilt, a quickening
current beating
beneath my feet.

No one spoke
the second day
as we watched
for Spottsville Bridge

waiting around a bend.
Everything was speeded up
though the river

had grown so
broad it hardly
seemed to move.
Then we saw
the bridge's piers
slicing the thick
brown water.

The raft turned
in the current
though four of us
struggled at the oars.
We hit
the center pier
broadside,

then hung
just a minute
while the pins
flew out like shot
and the bow
sheered off
with a splintering sound.

John, who hung
on the forward oar,
looked startled
then was gone,
while we swung free
and went on down,
our stern become our bow.

The bow logs
kept us company
as we were

swept along.
We entered the
mouth of the Green
and saw

the broad Ohio
before us
like a sea,
but could not stop,
caught by the falling
Ohio drawing
the rising Green.

Helpless we turned
in the current.
I feared we might
miss Evansville entirely
and be swept on to Cairo,
but the *Water King,*
prowling for rafts

caught in the
river's sudden fall,
threw us a line
and towed us
to Angel Landing
in the mouth
of Pigeon Creek.

We thawed ourselves
for a week
in Evansville's
warm embrace.
Though Lou
had not his hand
nor John
his life,

it was only 1917,
and the trees still
were endless
stretching through
the bottoms
far beyond
our sight.

Photo by Jeannie A. Survant

Joe Survant teaches poetry writing and literature at Western Kentucky University in Bowling Green, Kentucky. He has also taught at the University of Kentucky and at the Universiti Sains Malaysia, where he was a Fulbright Fellow. He is the author of *The Presence of Snow in the Tropics* (2001); *Anne and Alpheus, 1842–1882* (1996), winner of the Arkansas Poetry Award; and a chapbook, *We Will All Be Changed* (1995). *Anne and Alpheus* and *Rafting Rise* are the first two books of a planned Kentucky trilogy.

Contemporary Poetry Series
University of Central Florida

Mary Adams, *Epistles from the Planet Photosynthesis*
Diane Averill, *Branches Doubled Over with Fruit*
Tony Barnstone, *Impure*
Jennifer Bates, *The First Night Out of Eden*
George Bogin, *In a Surf of Strangers*
Van K. Brock, *The Hard Essential Landscape*
Jean Burden, *Taking Light from Each Other*
Lynn Butler, *Planting the Voice*
Cathleen Calbert, *Lessons in Space*
Daryl Ngee Chinn, *Soft Parts of the Back*
Robert Cooperman, *In the Household of Percy Bysshe Shelley*
Rebecca McClanahan Devet, *Mother Tongue*
Rebecca McClanahan Devet, *Mrs. Houdini*
Gerald Duff, *Calling Collect*
Malcolm Glass, *Bone Love*
Barbara L. Greenberg, *The Never-Not Sonnets*
Susan Hartman, *Dumb Show*
Lola Haskins, *Forty-four Ambitions for the Piano*
Lola Haskins, *Planting the Children*
William Hathaway, *Churlsgrace*
William Hathaway, *Looking into the Heart of Light*
Michael Hettich, *A Small Boat*
Ted Hirschfield, *Middle Mississippians: Encounters with the Prehistoric Amerindians*
Roald Hoffmann, *Gaps and Verges*
Roald Hoffmann, *The Metamict State*
Greg Johnson, *Aid and Comfort*
Markham Johnson, *Collecting the Light*
Hannah Kahn, *Time, Wait*
Sharon Kraus, *Strange Land*
Susan McCaslin, *Flying Wounded*
Michael McFee, *Plain Air*
Judy Rowe Michaels, *The Forest of Wild Hands*
Richard Michelson, *Tap Dancing for the Relatives*
Judith Minty, *Dancing the Fault*
David Posner, *The Sandpipers*
Nicholas Rinaldi, *We Have Lost Our Fathers*
CarolAnn Russell, *The Red Envelope*
Don Schofield, *Approximately Paradise*
Penelope Schott, *Penelope: The Story of the Half-Scalped Woman*
Robert Siegel, *In a Pig's Eye*

Edmund Skellings, *Face Value*
Edmund Skellings, *Heart Attacks*
Floyd Skloot, *Music Appreciation*
Ron Smith, *Running Again in Hollywood Cemetery*
Susan Snively, *The Undertow*
Katherine Soniat, *Cracking Eggs*
Don Stap, *Letter at the End of Winter*
Joe Survant, *Rafting Rise*
Rawdon Tomlinson, *Deep Red*
Irene Willis, *They Tell Me You Danced*
Robley Wilson, *Everything Paid For*
John Woods, *Black Marigolds*

Printed in the United States
1350300001B/277-618